ALL ABOUT
DAD

insights, thoughts, and life lessons
on fatherhood

Edited by **DAHLIA PORTER** and **GABRIEL CERVANTES**,
editors of *All About Mom*

adams media
avon, massachusetts

Contains portions of material adapted and adopted from *365 Reflections on
Fathers,* selected and arranged by Dahlia Porter and Gabriel Cervantes, ©1998,
F+W Publications.

Published by Adams Media, an F+W Publications Company
57 Littlefield Street
Avon, MA 02322
www.adamsmedia.com

ISBN 10: 1-59869-142-2
ISBN 13: 978-1-59869-142-9

Printed in Canada.

J I H G F E D C B

Library of Congress Cataloging-in-Publication Data
is available from the publisher.

This publication is designed to provide accurate and authoritative information
with regard to the subject matter covered. It is sold with the understanding that
the publisher is not engaged in rendering legal, accounting, or other professional
advice. If legal advice or other expert assistance is required, the services of a
competent professional person should be sought.
—From a *Declaration of Principles* jointly adopted by a Committee of the American
Bar Association and a Committee of Publishers and Associations

Many of the designations used by manufacturers and sellers to distinguish their
product are claimed as trademarks. Where those designations appear in this
book and Adams Media was aware of a trademark claim, the designations have
been printed with initial capital letters.

*This book is available at quantity discounts for bulk purchases.
For information, please call 1-800-289-0963.*

Contents

PART 1

FATHERS AND THEIR CHILDREN

Chapter 1

My Father

Every day of my life has been a gift from him. His lap had been my refuge from lightning and thunder. His arms had sheltered me from teenage heartbreak. His wisdom and understanding had sustained me as an adult.

—Nellie Pike Randall

My father . . . lived as if he were poured from iron, and loved his family with a vulnerability that was touching.

—Mari E. Evans

My father was two men, one sympathetic and intuitional, the other critical and logical; altogether they formed a combination that could not be thrown off its feet.

—Julian Hawthorne, of his father, Nathaniel

I remember being upset once and telling my dad I wasn't following through right, and he replied, "Nancy, it doesn't make any difference to a ball what you do after you hit it."

—Nancy Lopez

My fondest and earliest memory of my father is being able to get in his lap and sit. I still to this day sit in his lap, and he loves it. I don't think you're ever too old for that.

—Holly Heston, of her father, Charlton

He opened the jar of pickles when no one else could. He was the only one in the house who wasn't afraid to go into the basement by himself. He cut himself shaving, but no one kissed it or got excited about it. It was understood that when it rained, he got the car and brought it around to the door. When anyone was sick, he went out to get the prescription filled. He took lots of pictures . . . but he was never in them.

—Erma Bombeck

My dad is the backbone of our family. Any problem that I've ever had, he's always been there for me.

—Whitney Houston

The history, the root, the strength of my father is the strength we now rest on.

—Carolyn M. Rodgers

I modeled myself on my father. And this much at least was worthy of admiration: nothing downed his spirits for long.

—Elaine Feinstein

When I think of my father, the memories that bubble to the surface are not policy or politics. They are the man who opened a child's imagination, who taught her to be a good horsewoman and to always get back on when I fell off.

—Patti Davis, of her father, Ronald Reagan

I was not close to my father, but he was very special to me. Whenever I did something as a little girl—learn to swim or act in a school play, for instance—he was fabulous. There would be a certain look in his eyes. It made me feel great.

—Diane Keaton

To this day I cannot see a bright daffodil,
a proud gladiola, or a smooth eggplant
without thinking of Papa. Like his plants
and trees, I grew up as a part of his garden.

—Leo Buscaglia

Beaming like a lesser god,
He bounced upon the earth he trod.

—May Sarton, of her father

My dear father! When I remember him,
it is always with his arms open wide to
love and comfort me.

—Isobel Field

When someone who knew my father says I'm like him, I feel flattered. He was a shy, undemonstrative man, but good natured with a great, whimsical sense of humor.

—Paul Newman

When I was fourteen, my father was so ignorant I could hardly stand to have the old man around. But when I got to be twenty-one, I was astonished at how much he had learned in seven years.

—Mark Twain

My father died many years ago, and yet when something special happens to me, I talk to him secretly not really knowing what he hears, but it makes me better to half believe it.

—Natasha Josefowitz

My father didn't tell me how to live; he lived, and let me watch him do it.

—Clarence B. Kelland

I guess the only thing that's important is that he was my father. He was some guy, my Dad. Some guy.

—Jack Lemmon

The memory of Papa—tall, dark-haired,
with a neatly trimmed mustache, smiling,
warm and loving—is still vivid in my
mind. It will never fade.

—Leo Buscaglia

What strikes me as odd now is how my father managed
to get across to me without those heart-to-hearts which
I've read about fathers and sons having in the study or
in the rowboat or in the car. . . . Somehow I understood
completely how he expected me to behave, in small
matters as well as large, even though I can't remember
being given any lectures about it beyond the occasional,
undramatic, "You might as well be a mensch."

—Calvin Trillin

Of course there were areas of
safety; nothing could get at me
if I curled up on my father's lap,
holding on to his ear with one
thumb tucked into it. . . . All about
him was safe.

—Naomi Mitchson

One night at about two o'clock in the morning my father
caught a man stealing bananas from our backyard.
He went over to the man with his machete, took the
bananas, cut the bunch in half and said, "Here, you can
have it." And then he said, "From now on, if you need
anything from the back of our house, come to the front."

—Chi Chi Rodriguez

There must've been hundreds of people
cheering at some of those track meets,
but my father's voice always found me.
A simple "That's it, kid" and my feet grew
wings.

—Madison Riley

I used to feel that all I ever did was take from
my father: "Dad, my heater's not working."
"Dad, I need help building the shed." "Dad, can
you lend me money for a car?" Now he has a
computer. Things are evening up quickly.

—Den Schlaf

Whenever I try to recall that long
ago first day at school only one
memory shines through: my
father held my hand.

—Marcelene Cox

> In my dreams
> my father is always kind.
>
> —Paul Gunn Allen

It was my father's hand that
opened wide
The door to poetry, where printed line
Became alive.

—Helen Bean Byerly

There are a couple of pictures of the two of us that are of great sentimental value. In one, he's holding a bat in his left hand and has me comfortably balanced on his right shoulder. Some of the photos may be faded, but the memories of the happy times we spent together will always remain sharp and clear in my mind.

—Dorothy Ruth Picone, of her father, Babe Ruth

As my poor father used to say
In 1863,
Once people start on all this Art
Goodbye moralitee!
And what my father used to say
Is good enough for me.

—Sir A. P. Herbert

My father was a romancer and most of my memories of him are colored I fear by an untruthfulness that I must have caught from him like one of the colds that ran around my family.

—Mary McCarthy

My father's sonorous voice brought Kipling's "great gray-green, greasy Limpopo River all set about with fever-trees" snaking right to the foot of my bed.

—Victoria Secunda

How would I describe my father? Cool. He's cool. He's learned. He knows a lot of stuff.

—Wynton Marsalis

My father used to say that we must surrender our youth to purchase wisdom. What he never told me was how badly we get cheated on the exchange rate.

—Morris West

My father was as compulsive and efficient as I am. At Saturday morning breakfast, he would give each of us a list of chores that we had to get done for the day before any free time. My mother would get very upset when she got a list.

—David Fissel

Down in the bottom of my childhood my father stands laughing.

—Tove Ditlevsen

I laughed once in my father's face,
and he laughed, and the
two laughters
locked like bumpers
that still rust between us.

—Linda Pastan

My father was the most dominant person in
our family and in my life.

—Jimmy Carter

Papa was a man of brimstone and hot fire, in
his mind and in his fists, and was known . . .
as the champion of all fist fighters. He used his
fists on sharks and fakers, and all to give his
family nice things.

—Woody Guthrie

He was generous with his affection, given to great, awkward, engulfing hugs, and I can remember so clearly the smell of his hugs, all starched shirt, tobacco, Old Spice and Cutty Sark. Sometimes I think I've never been properly hugged since.

—Linda Ellerbee

He [my father] also emphasized that a man's dignity lives after him; it's what you contribute to this world that matters, not what you take out of it. The essence of love is not to be loved but to give love.

—Ricardo Montalban, of his father

He was strong rather than profound . . . I often wonder about him. In my struggle to be a writer, it was he who supported me and backed me and explained me . . .

—John Steinbeck

My father was very strong. I don't agree with a lot of the ways he brought me up. I don't agree with a lot of his values, but he did have a lot of integrity, and if he told us not to do something, he didn't do it either.

—Madonna

He had the precious gift of being deaf when convenient. Many people took this for absent-mindedness, but it was rather his faculty for concentrating on what suited him . . . in order to grasp reality better he limited his perceptions to a few definite things.

—Jean Renoir

Father was never late. Indeed, punctuality was his eleventh commandment. He saw lateness as a signal to the boss that you didn't care about your job, a potentially suicidal misstep. "If you're to be there at seven," he lectured me, "you be there at six forty-five. And you don't go to the water bucket more than once an hour."

—Dan Rather

My dad was relaxed and casual and believed in living in the present and having a good time. He had a full life and enjoyed himself no matter what happened.

—Bing Crosby

There is magic in the moment, for when I open my eyes and see my sons in the place where my father once sat, I feel an invisible bond between our three generations, an anchor of loyalty linking my sons to be the grandfather whose face they never saw but whose person they have already come to know through this most timeless of all sports, baseball.

—Doris Kearns Goodwin

As for my father, few souls are less troubled. He can be simply pleased with us, pleased that we exist, and, from the vantage point of his wondrously serene old age, he contemplates our lives almost as if they were books he can dip into whenever he wants. His back pages, perhaps.

—Angela Carter

Chapter 2

Fathers and Daughters

When a father gives his daughter an emotional visa to strike out on her own, he is always with her. Such a daughter has her encouraging, understanding daddy in her head, cheering her on—not simply as a woman but as a whole, unique human being with unlimited possibilities.

—Victoria Secunda

There is something like a line of gold thread running through the man's words when he talks to his daughter, and gradually over the years it gets to be long enough for you to pick up in your hands and weave into a cloth that feels like love itself.

—John Gregory Brown

The most important relationship within the family, second only to that of husband and wife, is the relationship between father and daughter.

—David Jeremiah

In love to our wives there is desire, to our sons there is ambition; but in that to our daughters there is something which there are no words to express.

—Joseph Addison

Arthur always had his arms around [his daughter] Camera. When he talked about her, his face would light up like the stars in the sky. He showed more feeling for his daughter than I had seen him show his whole life.

—Horace Ashe

I've been trying to think of the last thing that awed me. . . . The only thing I can come up with is the birth of my daughter almost five years ago.

—Leonard Pitts Jr.

What joy upon the honored
sire must come
When showing forth the wisdom of his
child!
Lo, she is fair and pure and undefiled
Thanks, thanks to her, the gladness of his home!

—Rahel Morpurgo

The father of a daughter is nothing but a high-class hostage. A father turns a stony face to his sons, berates them, shakes his antlers, paws the ground, snorts, runs them into the underbrush, but when his daughter puts her arm over his shoulder and says, "Daddy, I need to ask you something," he is a pat of butter in a hot frying pan.

—Garrison Keillor

I can do one of two things. I can be president of the United States, or I can control Alice. I cannot possibly do both.

—Theodore Roosevelt

One word of command from me is obeyed by millions . . . but I cannot get my three daughters . . . to come down to breakfast on time.

—Viscount Archibald Wavell

The thing to remember about fathers is, they're men.

—Phyllis Diller

I know my weak points, but I've thought I was attractive since I was a girl because my father thought I was. He must have been kind. I was always cute, but I was a butterball.

—Dana Delany

He wrapped his little daughter in his large
Man's doublet, careless did it fit or no.

—Elizabeth Barrett Browning

It doesn't matter who my father was;
it matters who I remember he was.

— Anne Sexton

I have never been a material girl.
My father always told me never
to love anything that cannot love
you back.

—Imelda Marcos

When it comes to little girls, God the father has nothing on father, the god. It's an awesome responsibility.

—Frank Pittman

I remember being at a point below his knees and looking up past the vast length of him. He was six foot three; his voice was big. He was devastatingly attractive—even to his daughter as a child. . . . His voice was so beautiful, so enveloping. He was just bigger and better than anyone else.

—Anjelica Huston, of her father, John

You fathers will understand. You have a little girl. She looks up to you. You're her oracle. You're her hero. And then the day comes when she gets her first permanent wave and goes to her first real party, and from that day on, you're in a constant state of panic.

—Stanley T. Banks in the movie "Father of the Bride'"

I wanted him to cherish and approve of me, not as he had when I was a child, but as the woman I was, who had her own mind and had made other choices.

—Adrienne Rich

What a dreadful thing it must be to have a dull father.

—Mary Mapes Dodge

Fathers seem powerful and overwhelming to their daughters. Let her see your soft side. Express your feelings and reactions. Tell her where you came from and how you got there. Let her see that you have fears, failures, anxious times, hurts, just like hers, even though you may look flawless to her.

—Stella Chess

I want something from Daddy that he is not able to give me. . . . It is only that I long for Daddy's real love: not only as a child, but for me—Anne, myself.

—Anne Frank

Nothing is dearer to an old father than a daughter. Sons have spirits of higher pitch, but they are not given to fondness.

—Euripides

If Daddy must be dethroned for daughter to begin to accept him as merely mortal, so, too, must a father give up the idea that his daughter will forever be his worshipping little girl—a process that can be peaceful or, more often than not, turbulent.

—Victoria Secunda

She climbed into my lap and curled into the crook of my left arm. I couldn't move that arm, but I could cradle Ashtin in it. I could kiss the top of her head. And I could have no doubt that this was one of the sweetest moments of my life.

—Dennis Byrd, of his daughter

Fathers are what give daughters away
to other men who aren't nearly good
enough, so they can have grandchildren
who are smarter than anybody's.

—Paul Harvey

The father of the bride is a pitiable
creature . . . always in the way—a
sort of backward child—humored
but not participating in the big
decisions.

—Dean Acheson

The meaningful role of the father of the bride was played
out long before the church music began. It stretched across
those years of infancy and puberty, adolescence and
young adulthood. That's when she needs you at her side.

—Tom Brokaw

Many fathers waste hours of precious time in the vain attempt to convince their daughters they shouldn't care what the boys think. They say things like, "You've got plenty of time for boys later." Come on. Get real, Dad.

—Nicky Marone

A father is always making his baby into a little woman. And when she is a woman he turns her back again.

—Enid Bagnold

It isn't that I'm a weak father, it's just that she's a strong daughter.

—Henry Fonda

Old as she was, she still missed her daddy sometimes.

—Gloria Naylor

Women's childhood relationships with their fathers are important to them all their lives.

—Stella Chess

What matters to me is not how I look, but the person inside, the one who grew up as—and is forever proud to be—the daughter of Bill Shepherd.

—Cybill Shepherd

Chapter 3

Fathers and Sons

The axe rang sharply 'mid those
forest shades
Which from creation toward the sky
had tower'd
In unshorn beauty. There, with
vigorous arm,
Walked a bold emigrant, and by his side
His little son, with question and response
Beguil'd the time.

—Lydia Howard Sigourney

Every father knows at
once too much and too
little about his own son.

—Fanny Fern

If you can give your son
only one gift, let it be
enthusiasm.

—Bruce Barton

I find that I'm moved by the silent memory of Dad and me silently competing at baseball on a dead-end street in a backwater Jersey town. There is something clean and elastic about it, and I look forward to speaking that mute language of men with my own son.

—William Plummer

The sooner you treat your son as a man, the sooner he will be one.

—John Dryden

He that does not bring up his son to some honest calling and employment, brings him up to be a thief.

—Jewish proverb

Most fathers would rather
see their sons dead
than either cultivated or
devout.

—Louis Auchincloss

You don't raise heroes, you
raise sons. And if you treat
them like sons, they'll turn
out to be heroes, even if it's
just in your own eyes.

—Walter Schirra Jr.

Every parent is at some time the father of the
unreturned prodigal, with nothing to do but keep his
house open to hope.

—John Ciardi

For rarely are sons similar to their fathers: most are worse, and a few are better than their fathers.

—Homer

We think our fathers fools, so wise
we grow;
Our wiser sons, no doubt, will
think us so.

—Alexander Pope

Having a child ends forever a man's boyhood, if not his boyishness. Having a child means that the son has, in a real sense, become his father. Sons are for fathers the twice told tale.

—Victoria Secunda

He may be president, but he still comes home and swipes my socks.

—Joseph P. Kennedy (on his son, John)

Fathers and sons are much more considerate of one another than mothers and daughters.

—Friedrich Nietzsche

When a father gives to his son, both laugh; when a son gives to his father, both cry.

—Jewish Proverb

I recently turned fifty, which is young
for a tree, midlife for an elephant, and
ancient for a quarter miler, whose son
now says, "Dad, I just can't run the
quarter with you anymore unless I bring
something to read."

—Bill Cosby

A man knows when he is growing old because he begins
to look like his father.

—Gabriel García Márquez

There must always be a struggle
between a father and son, while
one aims at power and the other at
independence.

—Samuel Johnson

My son, a perfect little boy of five years and three months, had ended his earthly life. You can never sympathize with me; you can never know how much of me such a young child can take away. A few weeks ago I accounted myself a very rich man, and now the poorest of all.

—Ralph Waldo Emerson, on the death of his son

No man is responsible for his father. That is entirely his mother's affair.

—Margaret Turnbull

Nearly every man is a firm believer in heredity until his son makes a fool of himself.

—Herbert V. Prochnow

It is funny. The two things men are most proud of are the things that any man can do, and does in the same way—being drunk and being the father of their son.

—Gertrude Stein

Why are men reluctant to become fathers? They aren't through being children.

—Cindy Garner

A father is much more than a human being to his son.

—Thomas William Simpson

To a young boy, the father is a giant from whose shoulders you can see forever.

—Perry Garfinkel

Tis happy for him, that his father was before him.

—Jonathan Swift

He that will have his son have respect for him and his orders must himself have a great reverence for his son.

—John Locke

The father who does not teach his son his duties is equally guilty with the son who neglects them.

—Confucius

Sir Walter, being strangely surprised and put out of his countenance at so great a table, gives his son a damned blow over the face. His son, as rude as he was, would not strike his father, but strikes the gentleman that sat next to him and said, "Box about: 'twill come to my father anon."

—John Aubrey

If the relationship of father to son could really be reduced to biology, the whole earth would blaze with the glory of fathers and sons.

—James Baldwin

Perhaps host and guest is the happiest relation for father and son.

—Evelyn Waugh

His father watched him across the gulf of years, which always must divide a father from his son.

—J. P. Marquand

The time not to become a father is eighteen years before a world war.

—E. B. White

In peace the sons bury the fathers, but in war the fathers bury the sons.

—Croesus

> For thousands of years, fathers and sons have stretched wistful hands across the canyon of time.
>
> —Alan Valentine

Leontine: An only son, sir, might expect more indulgence.
Croaker: An only father, sir, might expect more obedience.

—Oliver Goldsmith

Sons have always a rebellious wish
to be disillusioned by that which
charmed their fathers.

—Aldous Huxley

A man's desire for a son is usually nothing but
the wish to duplicate himself in order that such a
remarkable pattern may not be lost to the world.

—Helen Rowland

What was silent in the father speaks in the son; and often
I found the son the unveiled secret of the father.

—Friedrich Nietzsche

My father, when he went,
made my childhood a gift of a
half a century.

—Antonio Porchia

He followed in his father's footsteps,
but his gait was somewhat erratic.

—Nicola Bentley

The worst misfortune that can happen
to an ordinary man is to have an
extraordinary father.

—Austin O'Malley

Dad, you couldn't have done it better. You're actually pretty amazing especially because I'm fully aware of the demanding brat I was.

—John Travolta (in a letter to his father)

We were walking through the woods—I was no more than eight—when a branch snapped back and hit my face. As I started to bawl, my father got a disgusted look and said "You'll never make a Marine." . . . After that moment he realized his path might not be mine, he was the most caring and supportive man I have ever known.

—Jack Finley

For a boy to reach adulthood feeling that he knows his father, his father must allow his emotions to be visible— hardly an easy task when most males grow up being either subtly or openly taught that this is not acceptable behavior. A father must teach his son that masculinity and feelings go hand in hand.

—Kyle Pruett

Until you have a son of your own . . . you will never know the joy, the love beyond feeling that resonates in the heart of a father as he looks upon his son.

—Kent Nerburn

It is not flesh and blood but the heart
that makes us fathers and sons.

—Friedrich von Schiller

It was a big deal one day long ago in August when
your father had cleaned his finger nails for the
occasion and then you made him the proudest Dad
in all the world. Every boy was supposed to come
into the world equipped with a father whose prime
function was to be our father and show us how
to be men. He can escape us, but we can never
escape him. Present or absent, dead or alive, real
or imagined, our father is the main man in our
masculinity.

—Frank Pittman

Chapter 4

Children

It was then that I glimpsed the baby's head for the first time. . . . It was still a mere dot, but for me it was a spot of eternity.

—Carl Jones

Babies don't need fathers, but mothers do. Someone who is taking care of a baby needs to be taken care of.

—Amy Heckerling

I know fame and power are for the birds. But then suddenly life comes into focus for me. And, ah, there stand my kids. I love them.

—Lee Iacocca

The fundamental defect with fathers is that they want their children to be a credit to them.

—Bertrand Russell

Sometimes the poorest man leaves his children the richest inheritance.

—Ruth E. Renkel

"I never could suffer infants, but this kid is different than all I've seen," is an expression often heard from proud young fathers.

—Miles Franklin

I believe that what we become depends on what our fathers teach us at odd moments, when they aren't trying to teach us.

—Umberto Eco

We have to give ourselves—men in particular—permission to really be with and get to know our children. The premise is that taking care of kids can be a pain in the ass, and it is frustrating and agonizing, but also gratifying and enjoyable. When a little kid says, "I love you, Daddy," or cries and you comfort her or him, life becomes a richer experience.

—Anonymous

By the time a man realizes that maybe his father was right, he usually has a son who thinks he's wrong.

—Charles Wadworth

There's no pillow quite so soft as a father's strong shoulder.

—Richard L. Evans

Before I got married I had six theories on children; now I have six children and no theories.

—John Wilmot

A man never stands as tall as when he kneels to help a child.

—Knights of Pythagoras

Then I discovered that my son had learned something new. For the first time, he was able to give a proper kiss, puckering up his lips and enfolding my face in his arms. "Kees Dada," he said as he bussed me on the nose and cheeks. No amount of gratification at work could have compensated for that moment.

—Donald H. Bell

A man finds out what is meant by a spitting image when he tries to feed cereal to his infant.

—Imogene Fay

Dad taught me everything I know.
Unfortunately, he didn't teach me
everything he knows.

—Al Unser Jr.

One father can support twelve children,
but twelve children cannot support one
father.

—French proverb

A new father quickly learns that his child invariably
comes to the bathroom at precisely the times when he's
in there, as if he needed company. The only way for this
father to be certain of bathroom privacy is to shave at the
gas station.

—Bill Cosby

If you know his father and
grandfather you may trust his son.

—Moroccan proverb

It is a wise father that knows his
own child.

—William Shakespeare

It is a wise child that owes his own
father.

—Carolyn Wells

It is easier for a father to have children than for children to have a real father.

—Pope John XXIII

The debt of gratitude we owe our mother and father goes forward, not backward. What we owe our parents is the bill presented to us by our children.

—Nancy Friday

The roaring of the wind is my wife and the stars through the window pane are my children.

—John Keats

The gods visit the sins of the fathers upon the children.

—Euripides

> Almost every time I watch my daughters
> playing near me, especially in a physical
> way, an unusual feeling takes hold of me.
> I do not identify with the big smiling male
> whose offspring play at his feet, although
> I do expect to feel like this, looking at their
> tiny bodies and my own big one. On the
> contrary, I feel small and open. I feel as if
> the three of us are learning independently
> how to be dependent on one another.

—Mordechai Rimor

Men just don't "get" that the reason to become involved is for ourselves. Doing more with our children won't simply make women happier or keep them "off our back," but will create a deeper, more positive connection with the kids.

—Ron Taffel

The most important thing a father can do for his children is to love their mother.

—Theodore Hesburgh

A little child, a limbering elf singing, dancing to itself. . . . Make such a vision to the sight, as fills a father's eyes with light.

—Samuel Taylor Coleridge

Not only do our wives need our support, but our children need our deep involvement in their lives. If this period [the early years] of primitive needs and primitive care-taking passes without us, it is lost forever. We can be involved in other ways, but never again on this profoundly intimate level.

—Augustus Y. Napier

The first handshake in life is the greatest of all: the clasp of an infant's fist around a parent's finger.

—Mark Beltaire

Safe, for a child, is his father's hand, holding him tight.

—Marion C. Garretty

Of all nature's gifts to the
human race, what is sweeter to
a man than his children?

—Cicero

To show a child what has once delighted you,
to find the child's delight added to your own,
so that there is now a double delight seen in
the glow of trust and affection,
this is happiness.

—J. B. Priestly

Daddy's favorite tools are numbered among a child's favorite toys. Every kid wants to get her hands on Dad's retracting tape measure and his hammer. One father told me that his kids had taken over his under-car creeper as their favorite riding toy and he has trouble getting it back when he wants to change the oil.

—St. Claire Adams Sullivan

How can one say no to a child? How can one be anything but a slave to one's own flesh and blood?

—Henry Miller

Buying a stereo is merely a father's practice for the Big Buy: a car. When a child requests a car, a father will wish that he were a member of some sect that hasn't gone beyond the horse.

—Bill Cosby

A child enters your home and for the next twenty years make so much noise you can hardly stand it. The child departs, leaving the house so silent, you think you are going mad.

—John Andrew Holmes

Allow children to be happy in their own way, for what better way will they ever find?

—Samuel Johnson

I have found that the best way to give advice to your children is to find out what they want and then advise them to do it.

—Harry S. Truman

Don't demand respect, as a parent. Demand civility and insist on honesty. But respect is something you must earn—with kids as well as adults.

—William Attwood

More broadly across time and cultures, it seems, one perennial piece of advice to fathers has been the importance of acting tenderly toward their children.

—David Blankenhorn

The best brought up children are those
who have seen their parents as they are.
Hypocrisy is not the parents' first duty.

—George Bernard Shaw

When children sound silly, you will
always find that it is in imitation of their
elders.

—Ernest Dimnet

Raising children is part joy
and part guerilla warfare.

—Ed Asner

Parents ought, through their own behavior and the values by which they live, to provide direction for their children. But they need to rid themselves of the idea that there are surefire methods which, when well applied, will produce certain predictable results. Whatever we do with and for our children ought to flow from our understanding of our feelings for the particular situation and the relation we wish to exist between us and our child.

—Bruno Bettelheim

> Parents lend children their experience and a vicarious memory; children endow their parents with a vicarious immortality.

—George Santayana

Happy that man whose children make his happiness in life and not his grief.

—Euripides

We have seen that men are learning that work, productivity, and marriage may be very important parts of life, but they are not its whole cloth. The rest of the fabric is made of nurturing relationships, especially those with children—relationships which are intimate, trusting, humane, complex, and full of care.

—Kyle D. Pruett

Romance fails us and so do friendships,
but the relationship of parent and child,
less noisy than all others, remains
indelible and indestructible, the strongest
relationship on earth.

—Theodore Reik

When you have children, you begin
to understand what you owe your
parents.

—Japanese proverb

Children aren't happy with nothing to ignore,
and that is what parents are created for.

—Ogden Nash

A baby has a way of making a man out of his father and a boy out of his grandfather.

—Angie Papadakis

How pleasant it is for a father to sit at his child's table. It is like an aged man reclining under the shadow of an oak he had planted.

—Sir Walter Scott

PART 2

A FATHER'S LIFE

Chapter 5

Influence

There have been many times when I thought people might be better singers or better musicians or prettier than me, but then I would hear Daddy's voice telling me to never say never, and I would find a way to squeeze an extra inch or two out of what God had given me.

—Barbara Mandrell

What a father says to his children is not heard by the world, but it will be heard by posterity.

—Jean Paul Richter

My father got me strong and
straight and slim
And I give thanks to him.
My mother bore me glad and sound
and sweet,
I kiss her feet!

—Marguerite Wilkinson

None of you can ever be proud enough of being the child
of SUCH a Father who has not his equal in this world—so
great, so good, so faultless. Try, all of you, to follow in
his footsteps and don't be discouraged, for to be really in
everything like him none of you, I am sure, will ever be.
Try, therefore, to be like him in some points, and you will
have acquired a great deal.

—Queen Victoria

Words have an awesome impact.
The impression made by a father's
voice can set in motion an entire
trend of life.

—Gordon MacDonald

Today's sons can emulate Joe Montana,
Kirby Puckett, Wayne Gretzsky or Michael
Jordan. Yet Dad's way has some extra
appeal—he represents our personal destiny.
Few fathers will ever threaten Joe DiMaggio's
hitting streak, but to a son Dad's way far
outweighs social recognition.

—Jerrold Lee Shapiro

Many people now believe that if fathers are more interested in raising children than they were, children and sons in particular will learn that men can be warm and supportive of others as well as be high achievers. Thus, fathers' involvement may be beneficial not because it will help support traditional male roles, but because it will help to break them down.

—Joseph Pleck

Children have never been very good at listening to their elders, but they have never failed to imitate them.

—James Baldwin

I chance to talk a little wild,
forgive me;
I had it from my father.

—William Shakespeare

We live in the past to an astonishing degree,
the myth we live by, the presumptions we
make. Nobody can look in the mirror and not
see his mother or father.

—E. L. Doctorow

Setting a good example for
your children takes all the fun
out of middle age.

—William Feather

As a parent, you will often serve as an inadequate example to your child. A child will model himself after you in many areas: how you deal with frustration, settle disagreements and cope with not being able to have the things that you want, to name just three.

—Lawrence Balter

Even if society dictates that men and women should behave in certain ways, it is fathers and mothers who teach those ways to children—not just in the words they say, but in the lives they lead.

—Augustus Y. Napier

Children are natural mimics—they act like their fathers or mothers in spite of every attempt to teach them good manners.

—Anonymous

My father taught me to read from one of those first-grade readers. "Oh my," said Dick. "See Spot run." My father reacted right away, taking a bright red pencil, crossing out the "Oh my's" and writing in "Odds bodkins," "Gadzooks," "Gorblimey," and such all down the page. It was a revelation. It was the opposite of boring. The possibilities seemed endless and wonderful and I think it was at that moment I became a writer.

—Gordon Chaplin

By looking at us, listening to us, hearing us, respecting our opinions, affirming our value, giving us a sense of dignity, he was unquestionably our most influential teacher.

—Leo Buscaglia (from "Papa, My Father")

Why do I have to be an example for your kid? You be an example for your own kid.

—Bob Gibson

Chapter 6

Love

No man can possibly know what life means, what the world means, what anything means, until he has had a child and loves it. And then the whole universe changes and nothing will ever seem exactly as it seems before.

—Lafcadio Hearn

Love and fear. Everything the father of a family says must inspire one or the other.

—Joseph Joubert

There is something ultimate in a father's love, something that cannot fail, something to be believed against the whole world.

—Frederick W. Faber

My father used to play with my brother and me in the yard. Mother would come out and say, "You're tearing up the grass." "We're not raising grass," Dad would reply. "We're raising boys."

—Harmon Killebrew

> He loves his children not because everything in them is lovely and according to his liking, but because there is a real incomprehensible bond which is stronger than fiction.
>
> —Leroy Brownlow

A truly rich man is one whose children run into his arms when his hands are empty.

—Author Unknown

Men love their children, not because they are promising plants, but because they are theirs.

—Charles Montagu

I do not love him because he is good, but because he is my little child.

—Rabindranath Tagore

What children expect from grown-ups is not to be "understood," but only to be loved, even though this love may be expressed clumsily or in sternness. Intimacy does not exist between generations—only trust.

—Carl Zucker

The Fountaine of parent's duties is Love. . . . Great reason there is why this affection should be fast fixed towards their children. For great is that paine, cost and care, which parents must undergoe for their children. But if love be in them, no paine, paines, cost or care will seem too much.

—William Gouge

All the feeling which my father could not put into words was in his hand—any dog, child or horse would recognize the kindness of it.

—Freya Stark

When you are a father, and you hear your children's voices, you will feel that those little ones are akin to every drop in your veins; that they are the very flower of your life and you will cleave so closely to them that you seem to feel every movement that they make.

—Honoré de Balzac

Give a little love to a child, and you will get a great deal back.

—John Ruskin

In a man whose childhood has known caresses
and kindness, there is always a fibre of memory
that can be touched by gentle issues.

—George Eliot

Let us now praise famous men,
and our fathers that begat us.

—The Bible

My father gave me the greatest
gift anyone could give another
person, he believed in me.

—Jim Valvano

Dads don't need to be tall and broad
shouldered and clever. Love makes
them so.

—Pam Brown

Fathers! blessed word.

—Maria S. Cummins

It's only when you grow up, and step back from him, or
leave him for your own career and your own home—it's
only then that you can measure his greatness and fully
appreciate it. Pride reinforces love.

—Margaret Truman, (of her father, Harry S.)

To her the name of father was another name for love.

—Fanny Fern

My earliest recollections are of being dressed up and allowed to come down to dance for a group of gentlemen who applauded and laughed as I pirouetted before them. Finally, my father would pick me up and hold me high in the air. He dominated my life as long as he lived, and was the love of my life for many years after he died.

—Eleanor Roosevelt

Our father, while he lived, had cast magic over everything, for us as well as for her. He held his love up over us like an umbrella and kept off the trouble that afterwards came down on us, pouring cats and dogs!

—Mary Lavin

Be kind to thy father, for when
thou wert young,
Who loved thee so fondly as he?
He caught the first accents that fell from
thy tongue,
And joined in thy innocent glee.

—Margaret Courtney

No music is so pleasant to the
ears as that word—father.

—Lydia Maria Child

My father was an amazing
man. The older I got, the
smarter he got.

—Mark Twain

The best portion of a
good man's life,
His little nameless, unremembered acts
Of kindness and love.

—William Wordsworth

A man's fatherliness is enriched
as much by his acceptance of his
feminine and childlike strivings as it is
by his memories of tender closeness
with his own father. A man who has
been able to accept tenderness from
his father is able later in life to be
tender with his own children.

—Louise J. Kaplan

In the love of a brave and faithful man there is always a
strain of maternal tenderness; he gives out again those
beams of protecting fondness which were shed on him
as he lay on his mother's knee.

—George Eliot

It's a wonderful feeling when
your father becomes not a god
but a man to you—when he
comes down from the mountain
and you see he's this man with
weaknesses. And you love him
as this whole being, not as a
figurehead.

—Robin Williams

You don't have to deserve your
mother's love. You have to deserve
your father's. He's more particular.

—Robert Frost

Chapter 7

Discipline

Children need love, especially when
they do not deserve it.

—Harold S. Hubert

As a father I had some trouble finding the words to
separate the person from the deed. Usually, when
one of my sons broke the rules or a window, I
was too angry to speak calmly and objectively. My
own solution was to express my feelings, but in an
exaggerated, humorous way: "You do that again
and you will be grounded so long they will call you
Rip Van Winkle II," or "If I hear that word again, I'm
going to braid your tongue."

—David Elkind

It is a wise child that knows its own father, and an unusual one that unreservedly approves of him.

—Mark Twain

My father was frightened of his mother. I was frightened of my father and I am damned well going to see to it that my children are frightened of me.

—George V

I'll meet the raging skies, But not an angry father.

—Thomas Campbell

They were always reading the law to her at home, which might not have been so bad if her father and mother had read from the same book.

—Jessamyn West

When a father is indulgent, he is more indulgent than a mother. Little ones treat their mother as the authority of rule, and their father as the authority of dispensation.

—Frederick W. Faber

The best time to tackle a minor problem is before it grows up.

—Ray Freedman

The relationship of a parent with a teenager is shot through with ambiguities and hypocrisies, large and small—the child's dependance and resentment, the parent's self-indulgence and prohibitions. But somewhere within this uneasy mix, in the best of families . . . both parent and child know which lines should not be crossed; the child's sense of privacy, the parent's sense of propriety. A delicate balance preserved until, as adults, both sides can either laugh about it or forget it.

—Richard North Patterson

The thing that impresses me most about America is the way parents obey their children.

—Edward, Duke of Windsor

Most parents feel the keen embarrassment of having the infant misbehave . . . and they are apt to offer a tacit apology and a vague self-defense by sharply reprimanding the child in words that are meant to give the visitor the idea that they—the parents— never heard or saw such conduct before, and are now frozen with amazement.

—Agnes H. Morton

Always end the name of your child with a vowel, so that when you yell, the name will carry.

—Bill Cosby

Fathers are blind to the faults of their daughters.

—Proverb

How easy a father's tenderness recalled,
and how quickly a son's offenses vanish,
at the slightest word of repentance!

—Molière

Pronouncements have been raised to a fine
art by daddies, who use them to deflect a
messy personal encounter while keeping
everything under control.

—Signe Hammer

Govern a small family as you would cook
a small fish, gently.

—Chinese proverb

It is better to bind your child to
you by a feeling of respect, and by
gentleness, than by fear.

—Terence

An atmosphere of trust, love and
humor can nourish extraordinary
human capacity. One key is
authenticity: parents acting as
people, not as roles.

—Marilyn Ferguson

Chapter 8

Expectations

It is impossible to please the
whole world and your father
as well.

—Jean de la Fontaine

I phoned my dad to tell him I had
stopped smoking. He called me a quitter.

—Steven Pearl

Everyone expects to go further than his father went;
everyone expects to be better than he was born and
every generation has one big impulse in its heart—to
exceed all other generations of the past in all the things
that make life worth living.

—William Allen White

It is the family's expectations that will
make father into his best and biggest self.

—Samuel S. Drury

We criticize mothers for closeness.
We criticize fathers for distance. How
many of us have expected less from
our fathers and appreciated what
they gave us more? How many of us
always let them off the hook?

—Mary Kay Blakely

Noble fathers have noble children.

—Euripides

Fathers see babies as potentially grown-up—
they are more likely than mothers to transform
their perception of their newborn into fantasies
about the adult it will become, and about the
things that they (father and child) will be able
to do together when the infant is much older.

—Dorothy Burlingham

Fathers and mothers have
lost the idea that the highest
aspiration they might have for
their children is for them to be
wise . . . specialized competence
and success are all that they can
imagine.

—Allan Bloom

Every father
expects his boy to
do the things he
wouldn't do when
he was young.

—Kin Hubbard

Henry James once defined life as that predicament which precedes death, and certainly nobody owes you a debt of honor or gratitude for getting him into that predicament. But a child does owe his father a debt, if Dad, having gotten him into this peck of trouble, takes off his coat and buckles down to the job of showing his son how best to crash through it.

—Clarence Budington Kelland

The most important thing about our time together was this: whatever his politics or view of the role of women, he never made me think there was anything I couldn't do.

—Susan Kenney (of her father)

PART 3

FATHERHOOD
AND LESSONS

Chapter 9

The Need for a Father

Fathers have a special excitement about them that babies find intriguing. At this time in his life an infant counts on his mother for rootedness and anchoring. He can count on his father to be just different enough from his mother. Fathers embody a delicious mixture of familiarity and novelty.

—Louise J. Kaplan

Fathers represent another way of looking at life—the possibility of an alternative dialogue.

—Louise J. Kaplan

I cannot think of any need in childhood as strong as the need for a father's protection.

—Sigmund Freud

Our father presents an optional set of rhythms and responses for us to connect to. As a second home base, he makes it safer to roam. With him as an ally—a love—it is safer, too, to show that we're mad when we're mad at our mother. We can hate and not be abandoned, hate and still love.

—Judith Viorst

Children want to feel instinctively that their father is behind them as solid as a mountain, but, like a mountain, is something to look up to.

—Dorothy Thompson

Your children need your presence more than your presents.

—Jesse Jackson

Father, dear Father, come home
with me now,
The clock in the steeple strikes one;
You said you were coming right home from
the shop,
As soon as your day's work was done;
Our fire has gone out, our house is all dark,
And mother's been waiting since tea,
With poor Benny so sick in her arms,
And no one home to help but me.
Come home! Come home! Come home!
Please, Father, dear Father, come home.

—Henry Claywork

To tolerate the trend of fatherlessness
is to accept the inevitability of
continued social recession.

—David Blankenhorn

I believe that I'm letting my kids see that a man can be tender, sensible, warm, attentive to feelings, and present, just plain there. That's important to me, because I didn't get any of that from my own father, and I am realizing now how much I missed it.

—Anonymous

If fathers who fear fathering and run away from it could only see how a little fathering is enough. Mostly, the father just needs to be there.

—Frank Pittman

That is natural enough when nobody has had fathers they begin to long for them and then when everybody has had fathers they begin to do without them.

—Gertrude Stein

As a substitute father for hundreds of youths over the past thirteen years, I have yet to encounter a young person in difficulty whose trouble could not be traced to the lack of a strong father image in his home.

—Paul Anderson

The sound of his father's voice was a necessity. He longed for the sight of his stooped shoulders as he had never, in the sharpest of his hunger, longed for food.

—Marjorie Kinnan Rawlings

Chapter 10

Being a Father

By profession I am a soldier and take pride in that fact. But I am prouder—infinitely prouder—to be a father.

—Douglas MacArthur

I felt something impossible for me to explain in words. Then when they took her away, it hit me. I got scared all over again and began to feel giddy. Then it came to me—I was a father.

—Nat King Cole

A father is a person who is forced to endure childbirth without an anesthetic.

—Robert C. Savage

A man prides himself on his strength—but when his child is born he discovers that strength is not enough, and that he must learn gentleness.

—Pam Brown

I'd been cast in the part of my life . . . but I'd never heard of the leading man. I was definitely playing a supportive role; Lydia and I rated only feature billing. Still, I've never had a better part, and only once one as good—in the sequel. I was to be a father.

—Charlton Heston

Any man can be a father. It takes someone special to be a dad.

—Anonymous

Being a father
Is quite a
bother,
But I like it, rather.

—Ogden Nash

When a man has done his best, has given his
all, and in the process supplied the needs of his
family and his society, that man has made a
habit of succeeding.

—Mack R. Douglas

Like many fathers, he had a favorite ritual:
to put his whole family in the car and drive
somewhere. It didn't matter where—what
mattered was that he was behind the wheel.

—Signe Hammer

"Are you lost, daddy?" I asked.
"Shut up," he explained.

—Ring Lardner

He who brings up, not he
who begets, is the father.

—The Bible

What was it, this being "a good father"? To love one's sons and daughters was not enough; to carry in one's bones and blood a pride in them, a longing for their growth and development—this was not enough. One had to be a ready companion to games and hikes and outings, to earn from the world this accolade. The devil with it.

—Laura Z. Hobson

It is much easier to become a father than to be one.

—Kent Nerburn

To conceive a child, my father told me, is as simple as blowing a feather off your knee.

—John Cheever

Until you have a son of your own . . . you will never know the joy, the love beyond feeling that resonates in the heart of a father as he looks upon his son. You will never know the sense of honor that makes a man want to be more than he is and to pass something good and hopeful into the hands of his son. And you will never know the heartbreak of the fathers who are haunted by the personal demons that keep them from being the men they want their sons to be.

—Kent Nerburn

Don't make a baby if you can't be a father.

—National Urban League slogan

To be a successful father . . . there's one absolute rule: when you have a kid, don't look at it for the first two years.

—Ernest Hemingway

To become a father is not hard,
To be a father is, however.

—Wilhelm Busch

The good-enough father is not simply a knight in shining armor galloping to the occasional rescue; he is there through the good times and bad, insisting on and delighting in his paternity every pleasurable and painful step of the way.

—Victoria Secunda

Scary. That may be the most perfect word there is to describe what it's like to be a parent.

—D. L. Stewart

The pressures of being a parent are equal to any pressure on earth. To be a conscious parent, and really look to the little being's mental and physical health, is a responsibility which most of us, including me, avoid most of the time because it's too hard.

—John Lennon

The kind of man who thinks that helping with the dishes is beneath him will also think that helping with the baby is beneath him, and then he certainly is not going to be a very successful father.

—Eleanor Roosevelt

I loved those years of being Mr. Mom. One of the saddest days in my life was when Jennifer said, "Dad, I can wash my own hair."

—Billy Crystal

"Do you like being a parent—you know, being a father, having children and all?" Linnet once asked me. "Yes," I said, after a moment. "It's like dancing with a partner. It takes a lot of effort to do it well. But when it's done well it's a beautiful thing to see."

—Gerald Early

The daily arguments over putting away the toys or practicing the piano defeat us so easily. We see them coming and yet they frustrate us time and time again. In many cases, we are mothers and fathers who have managed budgets and unruly bosses and done difficult jobs well through sheer tenacity and dogged preparation. So why are we unable to persuade someone three feet tall to step into six inches of water at bathtime?

—Cathy Rindner Tempelsman

I don't want to be a good pal, I want to be a father.

—Clifton Fadiman

One father is more than a hundred schoolmasters.

—English proverb

Parents teach in the toughest school
in the world—The School for Making
People. You are the board of education,
the principal, the classroom teacher, and
the janitor.

—Virginia Satir

Dad, if you really want to know what happened in school,
then you've got to know exactly who's in the class, who
rides the bus, what project they're working on in science,
and how your child felt that morning. . . .
Without these facts at your fingertips, all you can really
say is "So how was school today?" And you've got to be
prepared for the inevitable answer—"Fine." Which will
probably leave you wishing that you'd never asked.

—Ron Taffel

There are three stages of a man's life:
He believes in Santa Claus, he doesn't
believe in Santa Claus, he is Santa
Claus.

—Anonymous

My dad was always there for me and
my brother, and I want my kids to have
the same kind of dad—a dad they will
remember. Being a dad is the most
important thing in my life.

—Kevin Costner

Sherman made the terrible discovery that men make about their fathers sooner or later . . . that the man before him was not an aging father but a boy, a boy much like himself, a boy who grew up and had a child of his own and, as best he could, out of a sense of duty and, perhaps love, adopted a role called Being a Father so that his child would have something mythical and infinitely important: a protector, who would keep a lid on all the chaotic and catastrophic possibilities of life.

—Tom Wolfe

The father is always a Republican toward his son, and his mother's always a Democrat.

—Robert Frost

Dads are stone skimmers, mud wallowers, water wallopers, ceiling swoopers, shoulder gallopers, upsy-downsy, over and through, round about wooshers. Dads are smugglers and secret sharers.

—Helen Thomas

There are to us no ties at all just in being a father. . . . It's the practice of parenthood that makes you feel that, after all, there may be something in it.

—Heywood Broun

Chapter 11

Fatherhood

I thought I never wanted to be a father.
A child seemed to be a series of limitations
and responsibilities that offered no reward.
But when I experienced the perfection of
fatherhood, the rest of the world remade
itself in my eyes.

—Kent Nerburn

Father!—to God himself we
cannot give a holier name.

—William Wordsworth

Fatherhood, for me, has been less a job than an unstable and surprising combination of adventure, blindman's buff, guerilla warfare and crossword puzzle.

—Frederic F. van de Water

Fatherhood is the single most creative, complicated, fulfilling, frustrating, engrossing, enriching, depleting endeavor of a man's adult life.

—Kyle D. Pruett

Fatherhood is pretending the present you love the most is soap-on-a-rope.

—Bill Cosby

I had heard all those things about fatherhood, how great it is. But it's greater than I'd ever expected—I had no idea Quinton would steal my heart the way he has. From the minute I laid eyes on him, I knew nobody could ever wrestle him away from me.

—Burt Reynolds

Fatherhood, like marriage, is a constant struggle against your limitations and self-interests. But the urge to be a perfect father is there, because your child is the perfect gift.

—Kent Nerburn

The advent of Father's Day in America has inspired the advertisement pages of the magazines to suggestions for brightening the life of this poor underprivileged peon. "Buy him an outboard run-about speedboat fourteen feet long with a sixty foot beam," say the magazines. "Buy him a synchromatic wristwatch, water and shock resistant. Buy him a fishing rod seven foot long with reinforced ferrules and large-capacity spinning Beachcomber reel," say the magazines, knowing perfectly well that if he gets anything, it will be a tie with pink horses on a blue background.

—P. G. Wodehouse

Everyone tells me that I've become much mellower since I became a father.

—Burt Reynolds

There are times when parenthood seems nothing more than feeding the mouth that bites you.

—Peter De Vries

Once you've been launched into parenthood, you'll need all your best skills, self-control, good judgement and patience. But at the same time there is nothing like the thrill and exhilaration that come from watching that bright, cheerful, inquisitive, creative, eccentric and even goofy child you have raised flourish and shine. That's what keeps you going, and what, in the end, makes it all worthwhile.

—Lawrence Balter

The power of this experience can never be explained. It is one of those joyful codings that rumbles in the species far below understanding. When it is experienced it makes you one with all men in a way that fills you with warmth and harmony.

—Kent Nerburn

Parenthood isn't a picnic. Dad may work from sun to sun, but as a father he's never done.

—William D. Wilkins

I looked at my daughters, and my boyhood picture, and appreciated the gift of parenthood, at that moment, more than any other gift I have ever been given. . . . Who else would think your insignificant and petty life so precious in the living, so rich in its expressiveness, that it would be worth partaking of what you were, to understand what you are?

—Gerald Early

Parenthood is not an object of appetite or even desire. It is an object of will. There is no appetite for parenthood; there is only purpose or intention of parenthood.

—R. G. Collingwood

My fatherhood made me understand
my parents and honor them more for
the love they gave.

—Kent Nerburn

Parenthood remains the single greatest
preserve of the amateur.

—Alvin Toffler

Paternity is a career imposed
on you without an inquiry into
your fitness.

—Adlai E. Stevenson

The toughest part of parenthood has nothing
to do with putting food on the table, clothes in
the closet, or tuition money in the bank. The
toughest part of parenthood is never knowing
if you're doing the right thing.

—D. L. Stewart

I was the same kind of father as I was
a harpist—I played by ear.

—Harpo Marx

If there's one thing parenthood has taught me it's
that naive mistakes do not bad parents make.
Bad parents have decidedly bad attitudes.

—John Rosemond

The American father . . . passes his life entirely on Wall Street and communicates with his family once a month by means of a telegram in cipher.

—Oscar Wilde

It has always been economically and politically important for men to know that they are the fathers of their children.

—Louise Bernikow

I won't lie to you, fatherhood isn't easy like motherhood.

—Homer Simpson

The most important domestic challenge facing the U.S. at the close of the twentieth century is the re-creation of fatherhood as a vital social role for men.

—David Blankenhorn

There was a time when a father amounted to something in the United States. He was held with some esteem in the community; he had some authority in his own household; his views were sometimes taken seriously by his children; and even his wife paid heed to him from time to time.

—Adlai E. Stevenson

Fatherhood ought to be emphasized as much as motherhood. The idea that women are solely responsible for deciding whether or not to have babies leads on to the idea that they are also responsible for bringing the children up.

—Shirley Williams

My father was often angry when I was most like him.

—Lillian Hellman

A father carries pictures where his money used to be.

—Anonymous

The ivory tower school of the men's movement has some strong feelings about the fatherhood role. According to its adherents, not only are men capable of upstaging women in baking banana bread and folding diapers, but nurturing, cooing, soothing, and everything short of breast-feeding should be included in the daddy repertory.

—Ira Victor

Sometimes my wife complains that she's overwhelmed with work and just can't take one of the kids, for example, to a piano lesson. I'll offer to do it for her, and then she'll say, "No, I'll do it." We have to negotiate how much I trespass into that mother role—it's not given up easily.

—Anonymous

Defining and celebrating the New Father are by far the most popular ideas in our contemporary discourse on fatherhood. Father as close and nurturing, not distant and authoritarian. Fatherhood as more than bread winning. Fatherhood as new-and-improved masculinity. Fathers unafraid of feelings. Fathers without sexism. Fatherhood as fifty-fifty parenthood, undistorted by arbitrary gender divisions or stifling social roles.

—David Blankenhorn

Chapter 12

Parenting

A man doesn't have to have all the answers—children will teach him how to parent them, and in the process will teach him everything he needs to know about life.

—Frank Pittman

Parenting is the one area of my life where I can feel incompetent, out of control and like a total failure all of the time.

—Anonymous

The father who would taste the essence
of his fatherhood must turn back from the
plane of his experience, take with him
the fruits of his journey and begin again
beside his child, marching step by step
over the same old road.

—Angelo Patri

It is a great moment in life
when a father sees a son grow
taller than he or reach farther.

—Richard L. Evans

Three stages in a
parent's life: nutrition,
dentition, tuition.

—Marcelene Cox

A king realizing his incompetence, can either delegate or abdicate his duties. A father can do neither. If only sons could see the paradox, they would understand the dilemma.

—Marlene Dietrich

Fathers are something else. They always give up their turn by saying something like, "Go ask your mother. She knows about things like that."

—Mary Kuczkir

Since mothers are more likely to take children to their activities—the playground, ballet or karate class, birthday parties—they get a chance to see other children in action. . . . Fathers usually don't spend as much time with other people's kids; because of this, they have a narrower view of what constitutes "normal" behavior, and therefore what should or shouldn't require parental discipline.

—Ron Taffel

To raise good human beings it is not only necessary to be a good mother and a good father, but to have had a good mother and father.

—Marcelene Cox

Becoming Father the Nurturer rather than just Father the Provider enables a man to fully feel and express his humanity and his masculinity. Fathering is the most masculine thing a man can do.

—Frank Pittman

Fathering makes a man, whatever his standing in the eyes of the world, feel strong and good and important, just as he makes his child feel loved and valued.

—Frank Pittman

No matter how calmly you try to referee, parenting will eventually produce bizarre behavior, and I'm not talking about the kids. Their behavior is always normal.

—Bill Cosby

Fathers should be neither seen nor heard. That is the only proper basis for family life.

—Oscar Wilde

If you are a parent it helps if you are a grownup.

—Eda J. LeShan

In a number of other cultures, fathers are not relegated to babysitter status, nor is their ability to be primary nurturers so readily dismissed. . . . We have evidence that in our own society men can rear and nurture their children competently and that men's methods, although different from those of women, are imaginative and constructive.

—Kyle D. Pruett

The guys who fear becoming fathers don't understand that fathering is not something perfect men do, but something that perfects the man. The end product of child raising is not the child but the parent.

—Frank Pittman

Although we consider parents the king and queen of a family, we think they must respect their subjects now, if only to avoid the guillotine later.

—Marguerite Kelly and Elia Parsons

Selective ignorance, a cornerstone of child rearing. You don't put kids under surveillance: it might frighten you. Parents should sit tall in the saddle and look upon their troops with a noble and benevolent and extremely nearsighted gaze.

—Garrison Keillor

If the new American father feels bewildered and even defeated, let him take comfort from the fact that whatever he does in any fathering situation has a fifty percent chance of being right.

—Bill Cosby

There are only two kinds of parents. Those who think their offspring can do nothing wrong, and those who think they can do nothing right.

—Miles Franklin

Anything which parents have not learned
from experience they can now learn from
their children.

—Anonymous

The mark of a good parent is
that he can have fun while
being one.

—Marcelene Cox

It will help us and our children if we
can laugh at our faults. It will help us
tolerate our shortcomings and it will
help our children see that the goal is to
be human, not perfect.

—Neil Kurshan

When I was away from home and missing my children, I asked myself why I didn't show my approval and enjoyment of them more when I was with them, when it would do them—and me—a lot of good. But I don't think I was ever able to take my own advice.

The psychological explanation for this is that we crabby perfectionists were started in that direction in our own childhood by the frequent criticism of our parents; it is very difficult to overcome the compulsion to repeat what was done to us.

—Benjamin Spock

Let children know you are human. It's important for children to see that parents are human and make mistakes. When you're sorry about something you've said or done, apologize! It is best when parents apologize in a manner that is straightforward and sincere.

—Saf Lerman

To maintain a joyful family requires much from both the parents and the children. Each member of the family has to become, in a special way, the servant of the others.

—Pope John Paul II

It seems to me that upbringings have themes. The parents set the theme, either explicitly or implicitly, and the children pick it up, sometimes accurately and sometimes not so accurately. . . . The theme may be "Our family has a distinguished heritage that you must live up to" or "No matter what happens, we are fortunate to be together in this lovely corner of the earth" or "We have worked hard so that you can have the opportunities we didn't have."

—Calvin Trillin

In colonial America, the father was the primary parent. . . . Over the past two hundred years, each generation of fathers has had less authority than the last. . . . Masculinity ceased to be defined in terms of domestic involvement, skills at fathering and husbanding, but began to be defined in terms of making money. Man had to leave home to work. They stopped doing all the things they used to do.

—Frank Pittman

So often, as the septuagenarian reflects on life's rewards, we hear that, "in the final analysis" of money, power, prestige, and marriage, fathering alone was what "mattered."

—Kyle Pruett

Chapter 13

Guidance:
What My Father
Taught Me

I watched a small man with thick calluses on both hands work fifteen and sixteen hours a day . . . a man who came here uneducated, alone, unable to speak the language, who taught me all I needed to know about faith and hard work by the simple eloquence of his example.

—Mario Cuomo, of his father

Parents have become so convinced that educators know what is best for children that they forget that they themselves are really the experts.

—Marian Wright Edelman

He always said, "Babe, pay your own way. Don't owe anybody anything." And that's the way I've lived.

—Lily Tomlin, of her father

I just owe everything to my father [and] it's passionately interesting for me that the things that I learned in a small town, in a very modest home, are just the things that I believe have won the election.

—Margaret Thatcher

Never get sick, Hubert, there isn't time.

—Hubert Humphrey's father

My father, who was in politics, told me to remain a bit mysterious. A good friend and father figure to him gave him this advice. It makes people wonder about you, draws them to you as we are all drawn to a mystery.

—Joe Mills

When I was a child my father taught me to put up my fists like a boy and to be prepared to defend myself at all times.

—Camille Paglia

A good name and good advice is all your dad can give you.

—Harry S. Truman

I remember my father's final lesson. My boy will learn by what I am and what I do far more than I will tell him.

—Norman Lewis Smith

I worked hard and made my own way, just as my father had. And just, I'm sure, as he hoped I would. I learned, from observing him, the satisfaction that comes from striving and seeing a dream fulfilled.

—Sigourney Weaver

My father was a statesman, I'm a political woman.

—Indira Gandhi

My father taught me to be honest, to do the best job I could do, and to be fair to whomever I was dealing with. Whenever I worked for anyone, he always insisted I see the job through. He would not let me quit until the job was finished. He taught me good manners and how to be a gentleman. After twenty-five years of marriage, I still hold the door for my wife.

—Harry Steele

Dad gave me two pieces of advice. One was "No matter how good you think you are, there are people better than you." But he was an optimist too; his other advice: "Never worry about rejection. Every day is a new beginning."

—John Ritter

Even if fathers are more benignly helpful, and even if they spend time with us teaching us what they know, rarely do they tell us what they feel. They stand apart emotionally: strong perhaps, maybe caring in a nonverbal, implicit way; but their internal world remains mysterious, unseen. "What are they really like?" we ask ourselves. "What do they feel about us, about the world, about themselves?"

—Augustus Y. Napier

My heart is happy, my mind is free
I had a father who talked
with me.

—Hilda Bigelow

Dad is sort of a laid back type, quiet and soft
spoken. He believes in a good education, being a
good person and having good morals. He instilled
those values in me.

—Ralph Brennan

Don't limit a child to your own
learning, for he was born in another
time.

—Jewish proverb

In my younger and more vulnerable years my father gave me some advice I've been turning over in my head ever since.

—F. Scott Fitzgerald

All that we [old poets] can do is keep our hearts as fresh as we may; to bear ever in mind that a father can guide a son but some distance on the road, and that how wisely he guides the sooner (alas!) must he lose the fair companionship and watch the boy run on.

—Sir Arthur Quiller-Couch

In order to live a good and clean life
my father has taught me six
basic rules:
If I don't do it, then you don't do it.
No one knows the truth but your
conscience and God.
You are never a failure as long as you
give it your best.
Do not forget your culture.
Do not do something just because
I am around.
Education and honesty are two of the
most important things that you
should have.

—Dagem Hailemarian

My best training came
from my father.

—Woodrow Wilson

Works Cited

Books

Adams, A.K. *The Home Book of Humorous Quotations.* New York: Dodd, Mead & Co., 1969.

Andrews, Robert. *The Columbia Dictionary of Quotations.* New York: Columbia University Press, 1993.

Bolander, Donald O. *Instant Quotation Dictionary.* New York: Dell Publishing, 1972.

Brussell, Eugene E. *Dictionary of Quotable Definitions.* Englewood, New Jersey: Prentice Hall, 1970.

Cohen, J. M. and M. J. *The Penguin Dictionary of Quotations.* New York: Viking, 1960.

Dad. Philadelphia: Running Press, 1997.

Edmonson, Catherine M. *365 Women's Reflections on Men*. Avon, Massachusetts: Adams Media, 1997.

Ehrlic, Eugene and Marshall De Bruh, eds. *The International Thesaurus of Quotations*. New York: Harper Collins, 1996.

Exley, Helen, ed. *The Best of Father Quotations*. New York: Exley Giftbooks, 1996.

Exley, Helen, ed. *The Love Between Fathers and Daughters*. New York: Exley Giftbooks, 1995.

Feuer, Susan. *For My Father*. Kansas City: Andrews and Mc-Meel, 1996.

Ginsberg, Susan, ed. *Family Wisdom: The 2,000 Most Important Things Ever Said About Parenting, Children, and Family Life*. New York: Columbia University Press, 1996.

Jakus, Elizabeth. *For Dad*. White Plains, New York: Peter Pauper Press, 1992.

Maggio, Rosalie, ed. *The New Beacon Book of Quotations by Women.* Boston: Beacon Press, 1996.

Magill, Frank N. *Magill's Quotation in Context.* New York: Harper & Row, 1965.

Margaret Miner and Hugh Rawson. *The New International Dictionary of Quotations.* 2nd ed. New York: Signet, 1993.

Mullane, Dierdre. *Words to Make My Dream Children Live.* New York: Doubleday, 1995.

Partnow, Elaine. *The Quotable Woman 1800–1981.* New York: Facts on File, 1982.

Partnow, Elaine. *The Quotable Woman Eve–1799.* New York: Facts on File, 1982.

Prochnow, Herbert V. and Herbert V. Prochnow, Jr. *A Treasury of Humorous Quotations.* New York: Harper & Row, 1969.

Safire, William and Leonard Safir. *Words of Wisdom*. New York: Simon and Schuster, 1989.

Simpson, James B. *Simpson's Contemporary Quotations*. New York: Harper Collins, 1997.

Warner, Carolyn. *The Last Word*. Englewood, New Jersey: Prentice Hall, 1992.

With Love to a Special Father. Grand Rapids, Michigan: Fleming H. Revell, 1995.

Web Sites

http://quotations.about.com/cs/specialdays/a/bls_fathers_day.htm

www.quotegarden.com/fathers.html

www.dadcafe.co.uk/articles/fatherhood-quotes.php

www.abundance-and-happiness.com/dad-quotes.html

www.quotationspage.com/subjects/parents/

What it means to be mom

ALL ABOUT
MOM

Trade Paperback, $9.95
ISBN 10: 1-59337-599-9
ISBN 13: 978-1-59337-599-7